GRACE IS FREE!

A LABORATORY SURVIVOR STORY.

(WORDS AND ART CREATED BY: JENNA CRAIG)

THIS BOOK IS DEDICATED TO ALL THE LABORATORY ANIMALS IN THE WORLD.

GRACE SENDS HER SUNSHINE.

YOU MATTER. THIS STORY IS FOR YOU.

CHAPTER ONE:

THE BIG BUILDING FILLED WITH PUPPIES...

HI, I'M GRACE.

I'M A BEAGLE, AND I LIVE WITH MY HUMAN MOM.

I LOVE HER SO MUCH,

AND I LOVE TO CURL UP NEXT TO HER

WHILE SHE WORKS ON HER COMPUTER.

MY LIFE IS WARM AND COZY NOW.

WHEN I'M NEXT TO MY MOM, I FEEL SO SAFE AND CALM.

SOMETIMES I FEEL SO RELAXED

THAT I FALL RIGHT TO SLEEP.

I HAVE LOTS OF TOYS AND MY FAVORITE STUFFED BEAR.

I PLAYED SO HARD WITH MY BEAR

THAT I ALMOST TORE HIS EAR OFF!

BUT I LOVE HIM JUST THE SAME.

DO YOU HAVE A FAVORITE BLANKET OR TOY?

I'M GRACE AND I LOVE TO BE WITH MY MOM.

I USED TO BE REALLY SAD, THOUGH.

CAN I TELL YOU MY STORY?

IT MIGHT ALSO MAKE YOU SAD AT FIRST,

BUT I PROMISE IT HAS A HAPPY ENDING.

IF YOU WANT TO HEAR MY STORY, RAISE YOUR HAND AND SAY:

"TELL ME YOUR STORY GRACE!"

AWESOME!

NOW GRAB A YUMMY SNACK IF YOU'RE ALLOWED TO,

SIT BACK AND GET COMFY.

CAN I TELL YOU MY STORY?

I WAS BORN ON A COLD WINTER DAY IN CUMBERLAND, VIRGINIA.
I CAME INTO THE WORLD IN JANUARY,
RIGHT AFTER CHRISTMAS.
I WAS BORN INSIDE A COLD STEEL CAGE.
MY CAGE WAS INSIDE A HUGE BUILDING
WHERE 4,000 OTHER BEAGLES JUST LIKE ME ALSO LIVED.

MANY BEAGLES HAD THEIR OWN STEEL CAGE,
BUT SOME BEAGLES HAD TO SHARE THEIR SMALL SPACE
WITH BROTHERS OR SISTERS.
THE BUILDING WE LIVED INSIDE OF
WAS FAR, FAR OUT IN THE COUNTRY
HIDDEN AWAY FROM VIEW.

I LIVED THERE FOR ALMOST THE FIRST YEAR OF MY LIFE.
I WILL TELL YOU ALL ABOUT IT
AND HOW IT MADE ME SO SAD.

NOW I LIVE A HAPPY LIFE WITH A GREAT FAMILY!
BUT IN ORDER TO HEAR MY HAPPY ENDING,
I HAVE TO TELL YOU ABOUT THE SAD STUFF FIRST.
BECAUSE I'M A SURVIVOR!

I LIVED WITH 4,000 OTHER BEAGLE DOGS IN A HUGE BUILDING WITH NO WINDOWS!

THERE WERE SO MANY BEAGLES
INSIDE THAT ENORMOUS BUILDING...
MORE THAN YOU'VE EVER SEEN IN YOUR LIFE.

WE DIDN'T HAVE ROOM TO RUN,
OR TO PLAY.
WE COULD NOT LOOK OUT A WINDOW.
WE COULD NOT SMELL THE GRASS OUTSIDE.
WE COULD NOT DO ANYTHING
BUT WAIT...
WAIT FOR SOMEONE TO COME SAVE US.

I WAS BORN INSIDE THIS BUILDING AND LIVED HERE ALL DAY EVERY DAY!

I'LL TELL YOU WHY
I LIVED IN THAT BIG SCARY BUILDING
WITH 4000 OF MY BEAGLE FRIENDS.
WELL.....SOME HUMANS
WANTED TO KEEP US IN THAT BUILDING
UNTIL WE WOULD BE OLD ENOUGH
TO BE LOADED INTO VEHICLES
AND TAKEN TO PLACES CALLED LABORATORIES.

CAN YOU SAY THAT WORD?
IT SOUNDS LIKE THIS:
LAB-OR-A-TORY.
LOTS OF MY BEAGLE FRIENDS HAD TO GO
WITH THE MEN TAKING THEM TO THE LABORATORY.

BUT I WAS NOT ONE OF THEM.
THEY DIDN'T TAKE ME.......YET.
I STILL HAD TIME TO BE SAVED. BUT WOULD I BE?
AND.....WHAT WOULD HAPPEN TO MY BEAGLE FRIENDS
INSIDE THE LABORATORY?

SOME OF MY BEAGLE FRIENDS
WERE TAKEN TO PLACES CALLED LABORATORIES.

LABORATORY WORKERS
DO SCIENCE TESTS ON BEAGLES.
THE TESTS HURT AND THEY ARE SCARY.
SOMETIMES THOSE HUMANS
TEST THINGS LIKE SHAMPOO ON MY BEAGLE FRIENDS
TO SEE IF IT WOULD BE SAFE FOR HUMANS TO USE.

HAVE YOU EVER GOTTEN SHAMPOO IN YOUR EYES
IN THE SHOWER?
IT STINGS SO BADLY.
THAT'S HOW MUCH IT HURTS
OUR ANIMAL FRIENDS' EYES TOO!

THE LABORATORY WORKERS THINK
IF THE SHAMPOO HURTS A DOG'S EYES,
IT WOULD HURT A HUMAN'S EYES TOO,
AND THAT'S HOW THEY DETERMINE IF IT
IS SAFE OR NOT.

BUT THAT'S SILLY!
DOGS ARE NOT HUMANS
SO WHY TEST ON THEM?

Testing laboratory
IF THIS SHAMPOO HURTS THIS BEAGLE'S EYES, IT'S NOT SAFE FOR HUMANS TO USE!
I WISH MY FRIEND GRACE WOULD TELL EVERYONE TO SHOP CRUELTY FREE.

NOT JUST BEAGLES ARE TESTED ON AND HURT IN LABORATORIES.

OTHER ANIMALS INCLUDE:

BUNNIES, RATS, MONKEYS, CATS AND PIGS TO NAME A FEW.

IF YOU DON'T LIKE ANIMALS BEING HURT IN TESTS,

YOU CAN HELP WHEN YOU GO SHOPPING!

NEXT TIME YOU GO TO A STORE TO BUY SHAMPOO AND OTHER BATH STUFF WITH YOUR MOM OR DAD,

HAVE THEM LOOK AT THE SHAMPOO BOTTLE.

THERE SHOULD BE AN IMAGE OF A LEAPING BUNNY!

(ON THE BACK OF THE BOTTLE)

THAT MEANS NO BEAGLES OR OTHER ANIMALS WERE HARMED TO MAKE SURE YOUR SHAMPOO IS SAFE.

LOTS OF OTHER PRODUCTS ARE TESTED ON BEAGLES TOO!

ALWAYS LOOK AT THE LABEL ON THE BACK.

THE PICTURE RIGHT HERE SHOWS YOU HOW.

THE BEST CRUELTY FREE LABELS SAY:

"CRUELTY FREE INTERNATIONAL"

-OR-

"PETA APPROVED".

CRUELTY
FREE
INTERNATIONAL

PETA
APPROVED

EACH YEAR, THOUSANDS OF BEAGLE DOGS LIKE MY FRIENDS
HAVE SCARY TESTS DONE ON THEM IN LABORATORIES
ALL AROUND THE WORLD!
AND THAT'S BECAUSE BEAGLES ARE SUPER NICE
AND WON'T USUALLY BITE BACK.
ISN'T THAT UNFAIR?

BACK TO MY STORY!!!........

IN THE BIG BUILDING,I SHARED MY CAGE WITH MY SIBLINGS.
WE DIDN'T HAVE A SOFT, COZY BED.
WE HAD TO SLEEP ON HARD FLOORS.
HAVE YOU EVER HAD TO SLEEP ON A FLOOR
AT A FRIEND'S SLEEPOVER?
IF YOU HAVE, YOU KNOW HOW UNCOMFORTABLE THEY ARE!

THAT WINTER WAS SO COLD THAT MY SIBLINGS AND I CUDDLED
TOGETHER TO TRY TO STAY WARM.
I WILL ALWAYS CHERISH MY SIBLINGS
FOR KEEPING ME WARM.
AND EVEN THOUGH I DIDN'T KNOW IT YET,
I WAS GOING TO BE OK.

IT WAS SO BORING
BEING IN OUR CAGE ALL DAY!

DAY AFTER DAY, FOR A VERY LONG TIME,
WE STAYED IN OUR CAGES WITH NOTHING TO DO.
WE FELT SO SAD, BUT WE TRIED TO TAKE NAPS
TO PASS THE TIME.

EVEN RESTING WAS DIFFICULT
BECAUSE THE BOTTOMS OF OUR CAGES WERE HARD.
OUR PAWS HURT FROM THE COLD ROUGH FLOORS.
WE ALSO WANTED TO RUN AND HAVE FUN,
BUT THE HUMANS KEPT US LOCKED INSIDE OUR CAGES.

WE COULDN'T TELL IF IT WAS RAINING OR SNOWING, OR SUNNY,
BECAUSE OUR ROOM HAD NO WINDOW TO LOOK OUT!

WE STAYED IN OUR CAGES WHEN IT WAS SPRINGTIME OUTSIDE.
WE STAYED IN OUR CAGES WHEN IT WAS SUMMER OUTSIDE.
WE STAYED IN OUR CAGES WHEN IT WAS FALL OUTSIDE.
WE STAYED IN OUR CAGES WHEN IT WAS WINTER OUTSIDE.
HOW WOULD YOU FEEL IF YOU COULD NEVER
GO OUTSIDE TO PLAY?
THAT'S HOW SAD WE FELT ALL THE TIME!

THEY WOULDN'T LET US PLAY OUTSIDE.

PEOPLE KEPT COMING IN MY KENNEL TO CLEAN
AND GIVE US FOOD AND WATER.
THE HUMANS JUST CAME AND LEFT.
THEY NEVER STOPPED TO TALK TO US, OR PLAY WITH US
.

IN THAT PLACE, I DIDN'T EVEN HAVE A NAME.
I HAD SIX LETTERS TATTOOED IN MY EAR.
THAT'S WHAT THEY CALLED ME.
DO YOU KNOW ANYONE WHO HAS A TATTOO?
MAYBE YOUR MOM, OR YOUR DAD...
OR MAYBE YOUR AUNT OR UNCLE?
DID THEY SAY THEIR TATTOO HURT THEM?
IT HURT ME TOO!

MY TATTOO SPELLED:
C N A C E L

ALL MY BEAGLE FRIENDS GOT ONE TOO,
BUT THEIRS HAD DIFFERENT LETTERS.
I WANTED A REAL NAME.
NOT JUST SILLY LETTERS
THAT DIDN'T MEAN ANYTHING!

THEY GAVE ME AN EAR TATTOO
WHEN I WAS 12 WEEKS OLD. IT HURT!

THIS IS ME ALL GROWN UP.
BUT MY TATTOO IS FOREVER.

CHAPTER TWO:
THE KIND STRANGERS WHO CAME TO RESCUE US

ONE DAY, WHEN I WAS SEVEN AND A HALF MONTHS OLD,
WHICH IS LIKE A GROWN UP IN HUMAN YEARS,
SOME PEOPLE CAME IN AND STARTED PICKING US UP.
WE FELT EXCITED, NERVOUS AND SCARED.....
ALL AT THE SAME TIME.
HAVE YOU EVER EXPERIENCED
ALL THOSE FEELINGS AT ONCE?

A KIND LADY SMILED AT ME,
AND A NICE MAN PICKED UP ONE OF MY SIBLINGS.
THEY SAID, "DON'T BE AFRAID. WE'RE GOING TO SAVE YOU.
YOU'RE SAFE NOW."

I LOOKED INTO THE LADY'S EYES AND I KNEW
SHE WAS TELLING THE TRUTH.
SHE SEEMED SO KIND AND CARING
AND EVERYTHING I ALWAYS HOPED FOR.
AND EVEN THOUGH I DIDN'T KNOW IT YET....
I WAS GOING TO BE OK.

I WAS NOT GOING TO BE SOLD TO A LABORATORY
BECAUSE THESE AMAZING HUMANS CAME TO RESCUE
MY BEAGLE FRIENDS AND ME!

NICE HUMANS CAME TO SAVE US!

THE NEXT THING I KNEW, ANOTHER KIND LADY CAME IN, PLACED ME IN A TRAVEL CRATE AND CARRIED ME OUTSIDE, WHERE A BIG VAN WAS PARKED!

I WAS SO NERVOUS AND DIDN'T KNOW WHAT WAS HAPPENING, OR WHERE I WAS GOING!
I COULD FEEL THE WARM SUN
THROUGH THE HOLES IN MY CRATE.
I COULD SMELL THINGS ALL AROUND ME.
THIS WAS MY VERY FIRST TIME BEING OUTSIDE!

THE NICE LADY SAID: "IT'S OK SWEETHEART. NO ONE IS GOING TO HURT YOU. YOU'RE GOING TO BE JUST FINE."
I WAS GOING FOR A RIDE IN THE VAN WITH OTHER BEAGLES
TO A PLACE IN AMERICA CALLED MICHIGAN.
IF YOU HAVE A MAP, YOU CAN FIND IT SUPER EASILY!
IT LOOKS LIKE A MITTEN!

OUR VERY FIRST TIME OUTSIDE!
OUR VAN WOULD TAKE US FROM VIRGINIA TO MICHIGAN.

CHAPTER THREE:

A ROAD TRIP IN THE "LOVE VANS" AND MY ARRIVAL AT A CURIOUS NEW PLACE

HERE IS THE ROUTE MY VAN TOOK.
WE STARTED IN A STATE CALLED VIRGINIA.
CAN YOU FIND IT ON THE MAP?

THE VAN DROVE ACROSS WEST VIRGINIA, OHIO
AND PENNSYLVANIA BEFORE REACHING MICHIGAN.
I SHARED THE VAN WITH LOTS OF OTHER BEAGLES.
IT WAS LIKE A FAMILY REUNION IN THAT VAN!
HAVE YOU EVER BEEN TO A FAMILY REUNION?

CAN YOU BELIEVE THAT SO MANY BEAGLES WERE RESCUED
BY THE NICE PEOPLE WHO RESCUED ME?
ALMOST 4,000 BEAGLES WERE RESCUED THAT DAY.
THAT'S A LOT OF DOGS!

OF COURSE, THEY DIDN'T ALL FIT IN THE VAN.
SOME HAD TO GO IN AIRPLANES.
THEY WENT TO DIFFERENT STATES ALL ACROSS AMERICA!
THAT WAS OK WITH ME.
I WAS JUST HAPPY WE WERE GOING SOMEWHERE SAFE.

DO YOU SEE THE ORANGE VAN
DRIVING FROM VIRGINIA TO MICHIGAN?
THAT WAS MY VAN!
I WAS ON A COOL ROAD TRIP
WITH A WHOLE GROUP OF OTHER BEAGLES.
THE AIRPLANES FILLED WITH OVER 3,000 OTHER BEAGLES
WENT TO THE OTHER STATES.

WE SAW SO MANY AWESOME THINGS ALONG THE WAY! TELL ME SOME FUN THINGS YOU DO ON ROAD TRIPS.

THE BEAGLES GOING TO MICHIGAN, INLUDING MYSELF... RODE IN A VAN. OUR VANS WERE CALLED "LOVE VANS" OR "LOVE BUS".

MOST OF MY FRIENDS
TRAVELED ACROSS AMERICA BY PLANE.

IT WOULD BE NEARLY IMPOSSIBLE TO SHOW 3,776 BEAGLES
IN THIS DRAWING.
HOW MANY DO YOU SEE HERE?

WHEN MY VAN ARRIVED TO MICHIGAN,
MY BEAGLE FRIENDS AND I WERE TAKEN TO ANOTHER SHELTER.
I WAS SO TIRED, BUT THIS PLACE FELT DIFFERENT....
AND MUCH NICER.

THERE WAS A BIG BACKYARD,
AND I GOT TO FEEL GRASS
FOR THE VERY FIRST TIME!
IT FELT STRANGE AND NEW UNDER MY PAWS.
ALL I HAD EVER KNOWN WERE COLD, HARD FLOORS.

THE GRASS WAS SOFT AND SQUISHY.
I KEPT LIFTING MY PAWS BECAUSE THE GRASS FELT FUNNY.
IT KEPT TICKLING ME AND I COULDN'T STOP LAUGHING!
DOES GRASS EVER TICKLE YOUR PAWS
AND MAKE YOU LAUGH?

WOW! THIS IS GRASS?
IT SMELLS AMAZING AND IT FEELS SO GOOD UNDER MY PAWS!

CHAPTER FOUR:

A LADY NAMED CHERYL AND THE CAR RIDE "HOME"

A FEW DAYS LATER,
WHILE I WAS
EXLORING THE BACK YARD
AT MY NEW SHELTER,
AND LEARNING ABOUT THIS NEW WEIRD STUFF CALLED GRASS,
ANOTHER STRANGE LADY CAME TO VISIT US.

SHE HAD REALLY GOOD VIBES
AND I COULD SENSE HOW COOL SHE WAS.
DO YOU KNOW DOGS CAN TELL
IF PEOPLE ARE NICE OR MEAN RIGHT AWAY?
SHE WAS SO NICE, SO I WALKED RIGHT UP TO HER
AND SNIFFED HER HAND.

SHE SMILED AND SAID EXCITEDLY:
"I'LL TAKE THIS ONE. SHE'S PERFECT!"
I WAS SO HAPPY I COULDN'T STOP WAGGING MY TAIL.
DID THAT MEAN...
SHE WAS GOING TO TAKE ME HOME?

I TRUSTED MY AUNT CHERYL RIGHT AWAY.

I RODE IN THE NICE LADY'S CAR, IN THE BACKSEAT,
ALL THE WAY TO MY MOM'S HOUSE.
I CRIED A LITTLE BECAUSE I WAS NERVOUS
AND DIDN'T KNOW WHERE I WAS GOING.
BUT THIS ADVENTURE FELT EXCITING,
IN A GOOD WAY.

WARM SUNLIGHT CAME THROUGH THE CAR WINDOW
AND FELT SO GOOD ON MY FUR.
THE LADY TALKED SOFTLY
AND PLAYED GENTLE MUSIC THE WHOLE WAY.
AND EVEN THOUGH I DIDN'T KNOW IT YET....
I WAS GOING TO BE OK.

FOR THE FIRST TIME IN MY LIFE, I FELT CALM
AND SAFE
AND REALLY HAPPY.
SOON ENOUGH, I LEARNED HER NAME WAS CHERYL.
SHE WAS MY MOM'S BEST FRIEND.
SHE IS MY AUNT CHERYL.
DO YOU HAVE AN AUNT THAT YOU LOVE?
WHAT IS HER NAME?

I FELT IN MY HEART I WAS GOING TO MY FOREVER HOME...

CHAPTER FIVE:

MEETING MY HUMAN MOM AND SISTERS... OH, AND SOFT BEDS ARE AMAZING!

AFTER A LONG DRIVE, MY AUNT CHERYL STOPPED THE CAR
AND GENTLY LIFTED ME OUT OF THE BACKSEAT.
SHE PLACED MY CRATE ON THE GRASS IN FRONT OF A HOUSE
AND THAT'S WHEN I SAW.....
MY HUMAN MOM FOR THE VERY FIRST TIME!

SHE KNEELED DOWN BY MY CRATE
AND THE MINUTE I HEARD HER VOICE,
MY TAIL STARTED THUMPING
AGAINST THE WALLS OF MY CRATE.
I COULDN'T CONTAIN MY EXCITEMENT.
HAVE YOU EVER BEEN SO HAPPY AND SO EXCITED
THAT YOU FELT LIKE YOU WERE GOING TO BURST OPEN
LIKE A BALLOON WHEN IT EXPLODES?
THAT'S HOW I FELT!

MY NEW SISTER FAITH, A SMALL BLACK CHIHUAHUA
WITH POINTY EARS,
GREETED ME WITH EXCITEMENT TOO.
I KNEW I WAS HOME FOR GOOD THIS TIME!

I WAS SO HAPPY TO MEET MY HUMAN MOM AND MY NEW SISTER FAITH...A TINY CHIHUAHUA.

THE VERY FIRST THING I DID WHEN I ARRIVED HOME
WAS SLEEP....AND SLEEP...AND SLEEP.
I WAS COMPLETELY EXHAUSTED.

I WAS RESCUED....
I TOOK A ROAD TRIP ACROSS AMERICA IN A VAN,
I STAYED IN A TEMPORARY HOME FOR A FEW DAYS,
AND I RODE IN MY AUNT CHERYL'S CAR
ALL THE WAY TO MY MOM'S HOUSE...
.ALL IN ABOUT A WEEK!

THAT'S A LOT OF ACTIVTIES FOR A LITTLE BEAGLE LIKE ME....
A LITTLE BEAGLE WHO NEVER WENT OUTSIDE
OR TRAVELED BEFORE!

I FELT SO SAFE AND RELAXED IN MY NEW HOME
THAT I COULD NOT KEEP MY EYES OPEN.
HAVE YOU EVER TRIED REALLY HARD TO STAY AWAKE
BUT YOUR EYES COULD NOT STAY OPEN?
I COULD FINALLY REST.
I FELT SOOO SLEEPY BUT ALSO SO HAPPY.

I NEVER HAD A SOFT BED BEFORE.
IT FELT SO WONDERFUL.

WHAT IS MY LIFE LIKE NOW THAT I'M FREE
FROM THAT BAD PLACE WITH NO WINDOWS?
MY LIFE NOW IS:
INCREDIBLE!
RELAXING!
FILLED WITH HAPPINESS!

MY MOM LIVES IN AN APARTMENT
WHERE THE SUN SHINES IN HER
BEDROOM WINDOW ALL DAY LONG!
I SPEND MY AFTERNOONS NAPPING ON HER COZY BIG BED
AND I CAN FEEL THE WARM SUNSHINE
COMING THROUGH THE WINDOW
ON MY BACK EVERY DAY.

I NEVER THINK ABOUT THE DARK, SCARY PLACE
WHERE I ONCE LIVED
AS A PUPPY.

NAPS ON MOM'S BED ARE MY FAVORITE.

AND EVERY NIGHT
WHEN IT GETS DARK OUTSIDE,
I JUMP ON MOM'S BED
AND WAIT FOR HER TO TURN ON MY STAR PROJECTOR.
IT MAKES ME SOOO HAPPY
TO BE SURROUNDED BY STARS
ALL OVER MOM'S ROOM.
THE CEILING AND WALLS ARE ALL LIT UP
AND IT'S SO BEAUTIFUL.

I FIND MY GALAXY LIGHT
SO RELAXING.

CHAPTER SIX:

ADVENTURES WITH MY FAMILY AND LOVING MY FOREVER HOME

I GO SO MANY PLACES WITH MY FAMILY
AND SEE SO MANY THINGS!
EVERY DAY IS AN ADVENTURE.

MY FAVORITE PLACE IN THE WHOLE WORLD
IS A LAKE IN THE WOODS IN NORTHERN MICHIGAN
WHERE I GET TO SWIM.

I'M AN EXCELLENT SWIMMER IF I DO SAY SO MYSELF.
THE WATER IS COLD AND REFRESHING
AND MY HUMAN DAD STAYS RIGHT BY MY SIDE
TO MAKE SURE I'M OK.

MY DAD AND I LOVE TO SWIM.
HE STAYS CLOSE TO MAKE SURE I'M SAFE.

BUT MY VERY FAVORITE PART OF BEING FREE

IS HAVING MY SISTERS BY MY SIDE.

MY CHIHUAHUA SISTER "FAITH" HAS A NICKNAME: PEANUT.

MY OTHER SISTER IS A DACHSHUND,

ALSO KNOWN AS A WIENER DOG. HER NAME IS DORA.

DORA IS OLD AND SOMETIMES GRUMPY

BUT I LOVE HER SO MUCH.

I CAN'T IMAGINE MY LIFE NOW WITHOUT MY SISTERS.

THEY ARE MY BEST FRIENDS.

LIFE IS SO GOOD.

BEFORE, WHEN I LIVED IN THE SCARY BIG BUILDING

WITH THOUSANDS OF OTHER BEAGLES,

I WAS FRIGHTENED AND SAD ALL THE TIME.

NOW, I HAVE NOTHING TO FEAR.

MY FAMILY IS ALWAYS RIGHT HERE WHEN I NEED THEM.

I CAN BE MYSELF AND JUST HAVE FUN.

I KNOW I AM TRULY LOVED.

I AM NO LONGER C N A C E L.

I AM GRACE. AND I AM FREE!

THE END.

MY SISTERS ARE MY BEST FRIENDS FOREVER.

MEET THE REAL GRACE AND HER MOM "JENNA"

GRACE WAS RESCUED IN 2022
FROM A BREEDING/TESTING FACILITY IN VIRGINIA.
SHE WAS 7.5 MONTHS OLD.
SHE IS NOW 4 YEARS OLD IN 2026.
GRACE & HER MOM HELP TO RAISE AWARENESS
ABOUT ANIMAL TESTING
ON HER IG PAGE: @GRACE_IS_FREE_
IF YOU'D LIKE TO WEAR CUTE FASHION
THAT SPREADS THE MESSAGE ABOUT ANIMAL TESTING
& ALSO DONATES A PERCENTAGE TO SHELTERS & LABORATORY RESCUES,
VISIT GRACE'S ETSY SHOP: GRACE IS FREE BOUTIQUE

SOME FACTS ABOUT

ANIMAL TESTING.....

EACH YEAR IN THE U.S., APPROXIMATELY 40,000 BEAGLES/DOGS ARE USED IN EXPERIMENTS.

MILLIONS OF MICE, RATS, HAMSTERS, CATS, GUINEA PIGS, GERBILS, FISH, NON HUMAN PRIMATES, SHEEP, PIGS, HORSES AND MANY MORE ANIMAL SPECIES ARE ALSO USED.

WHY ARE BEAGLES

USED IN ANIMAL EXPERIMENTS?

BEAGLES ARE NICE

BEAGLES ARE FORGIVING

BEAGLES DON'T COMMONLY BITE

BEAGLES ARE SMALL FOR CAGE HOUSING

HOW CAN WE HELP ANIMALS USED IN CRUEL TESTING

AND TEACH OUR NEXT GEN TO HELP THEM TOO?

SHOP CRUELTY FREE BY LOOKING AT THE LABEL!

HERE ARE SOME NAMES/LOGOS TO LOOK FOR
ON THE BACK OF THE BOTTLE OF:
HOUSEHOLD CLEANING/SHAMPOO/CONDITIONER/LAWN CARE-WEED KILLERS, FERTILIZERS, PESTICIDES/DISINFECTANTS/BATH AND BODY PRODUCTS/SOAPS/LOTIONS/HAIR SPRAYS/WINDOW/ FLOOR CLEANERS/LAUNDRY DETERGENTS, ETC..........

"PETA APPROVED"

PETA'S "BEAUTY WITHOUT BUNNIES"

THE "LEAPING BUNNY" PICTURE!

"CHOOSE CRUELTY FREE"

-I AM NOT ENDORSED, AFFILIATED WITH, PAID BY, OR SPONSORED BY PETA. I'M USING THIS INFO FOR EDUCATIONAL PURPOSES!

"CRUELTY CUTTER"

APP

FROM:

BEAGLE FREEDOM PROJECT.

IT'S A FREE APP

TO DOWNLOAD!

I'M NOT ENDORSED, AFFILIATED WITH, PAID BY, OR SPONSORED BY BEAGLE FREEDOM PROJECT. I'M USING THIS INFO FOR EDUCATIONAL PURPOSES!

BY PURCHASING CRUELTY FREE

PRODUCTS......

YOU WILL HELP REDUCE DEMAND

FOR PRODUCTS TESTED ON ANIMALS!

IT REALLY WORKS!

LOTS AND LOTS OF COMPANIES

ARE NOW CRUELTY FREE.

"I BELIEVE ANIMALS SHOULD BE RESPECTED AS CITIZENS OF THIS EARTH. THEY SHOULD HAVE THE RIGHT TO THEIR OWN FREEDOM, THEIR OWN FAMILIES AND THEIR OWN LIFE."

–JOHN FELDMANN

We hope our Gracie's story touched your heart.

www.ingramcontent.com/pod-product-compliance
Lightning Source LLC
LaVergne TN
LVHW070140110826
845147LV00002B/293

* 9 7 9 8 2 3 4 0 4 9 9 8 8 *